BACKYARD BEARS

BACKYARD BEARS

Conservation, Habitat Changes, and the Rise of Urban Wildlife

by AMY CHERRIX

Houghton Mifflin Harcourt

Boston   New York

THIS BOOK IS FOR MY MOM, MARTY KEENER CHERRIX:
COWGIRL, ADVENTURER, AND THE BRAVEST PERSON I KNOW.
I LOVE YOU. —A.C.

Houghton Mifflin Harcourt Books for Young Readers is an
imprint of Houghton Mifflin Harcourt Publishing Company.

hmhco.com

Book design by Andrea Miller
The text of this book is set in Chaparral Pro.

Library of Congress Cataloging-in-Publication Data is available.
ISBN 978-1-328-85868-9

Manufactured in China
SCP 10 9 8 7 6 5 4 3 2 1
4500721636

PHOTO CREDITS: Steve Atkins ii, iv–v, vi, 3–10, 11 (left), 13–18, 20, 21, 23, 25, 32,
35, 37, 39, 40, 45, 56–63, 65–68, 70–71; Marty Cherrix 49; *Citizen Times/USA Today*
i; Jacques Descloitres, MODIS Land Rapid Response Team, NASA GSFC 47; Steve
Evans 50; Nickolas Gould 22, 24, 31; Great Smoky Mountains National Park and the
Open Parks Network, Clemson University 27, 30; Tony Head 2; Nayan Khanolkaar
42–43; Library of Congress, Geography and Maps Division 52; Gary Mantle 51;
Melissa McGraw, NCWRC 11 (right), 12, 19; Florain Moellers 53; Twain Newhart 46;
Charles Sharp 54; State Archives of North Carolina 28–29; Jennifer Strules, North
Carolina Urban/Suburban Bear Study 33; Southeastern Association of Fish and
Wildlife Agencies 64

CONTENTS

Chapter One: A Close Encounter 1

Chapter Two: Consequences of Conservation 26

Chapter Three: A World Going Wild 43

Chapter Four: "What a Bear!" 56

Six Ways to Be BearWise 66

How to Behave in a Bear Encounter 66

Web Resources 67

Glossary 68

Notes 69

Selected Bibliography 71

Acknowledgments/Author's Note 71

Index 72

The sun rises over the foggy Blue Ridge Mountains of Western North Carolina.

CHAPTER ONE
A Close Encounter

MORNING DOESN'T COME easily to the Blue Ridge Mountains of Western North Carolina. An impossibly thick blanket of fog covers them in a near-constant swirl of gray. Sometimes it takes our solar system's brightest star half the day to vanquish the soupy mist. Once the fog evaporates, these mountains are a testament to the color blue. For centuries, their startling jewel-toned beauty has tempted countless doomed wanderers to stray from the relative safety of well-traveled mountain trails. And these hills are old. At 200 to 300 million years of age, they are among the oldest mountains in the world, once resembling the mighty Himalayas. The French Broad River snakes through them on a primordial riverbed barely younger than the Nile.

Before this land was cleared, paved, and dotted with hillside homes, it was densely forested terrain. There are legends of rhododendron thickets so large and twisted with age that lost travelers wandered in them for days. Even now—despite rapid development and rising populations in mountain towns such as the region's largest city, Asheville, North Carolina—a person can vanish into the tree line, just a few steps from the road. And although humankind still attempts to tame this old wilderness, first and foremost it has always belonged to the animals, including its black bears (*Ursus americanus*).

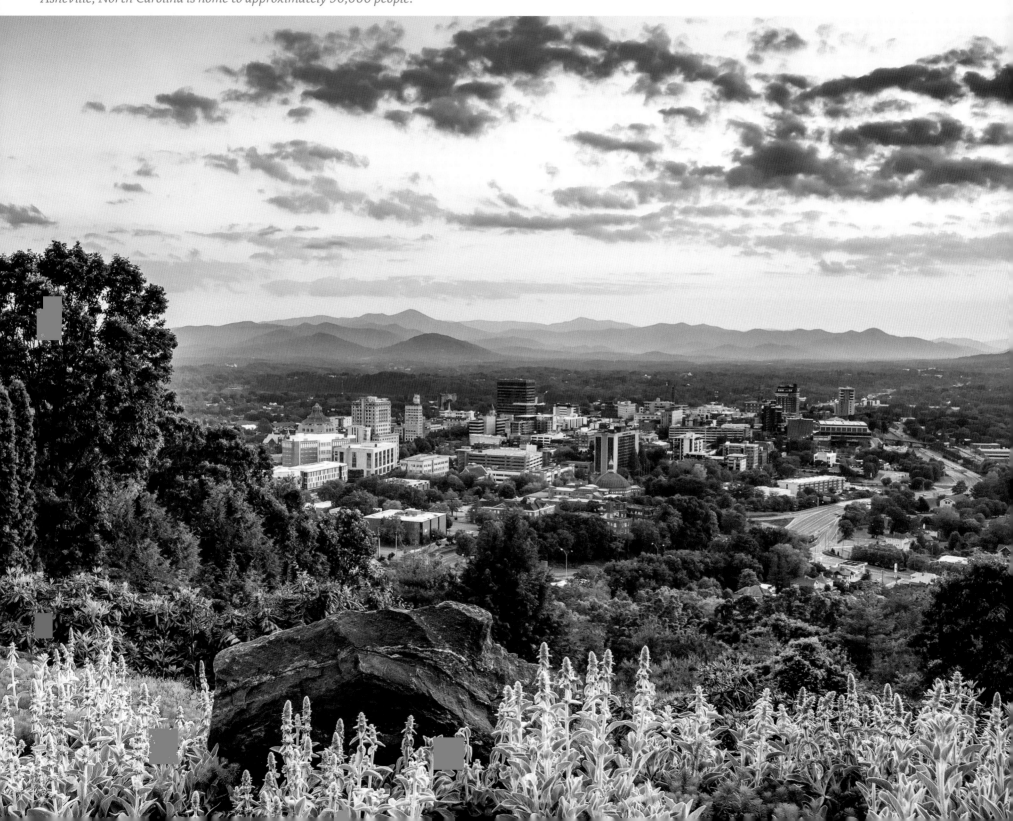

Asheville, North Carolina is home to approximately 90,000 people.

These days, however, Asheville also belongs to its human residents, many of whom are delighted by the bears but also wary of them. It's a balancing act for people like Rebecca Dougherty, who regularly encounters Asheville's urban bear population around her family home. She doesn't live in fear of the animals, but she does take the necessary precautions. "I've come across many bears," she says, "but I always do the wise and safe thing by slowly backing away." Rebecca says she respects the animals, but she also worries because there is a lot of misinformation about their behavior that can lead to trouble. "People mistakenly believe they will always be able to hear a bear before they see it. But I have found myself too close to a bear because I didn't realize it was nearby until I actually saw it. If I'm near the door of the house and I spot a bear, I step inside." In the past, she has also quickly stolen into her car until a bear moved along.

As people around Asheville have learned, when they live in close proximity with bears, it's up to them to be proactive about deterring bear activity. Sometimes that requires a little creative problem solving. Rebecca's family began by rethinking garbage disposal. One of their cleverest ideas was freezing their food waste. Rather than tossing it into an outdoor compost pile that might attract bears, they freeze it. On trash day, the frozen block of discarded food is packaged with the other trash and taken out to the curb shortly before it's scheduled for collection. "We make an effort to shoo them away," Rebecca says. "We don't want them to get too comfy here."

The number of black bears in and around Asheville is growing. There are between 15,000 and 20,000 black bears statewide, approximately 7,000 of which live throughout Western North Carolina. As additional land is developed to create new neighborhoods, people are moving closer to where the bears live, increasing the chance of human interaction with these animals, who are highly capable of adapting to life near people. And though hunting is the primary method for managing the bear population, it is not allowed in Asheville. This, combined with successful conservation efforts and the proximity of black bear habitat, has resulted in urbanized black bears living within city limits. Of the hundred counties in North Carolina, approximately 41 percent of all phone calls about bears come from Buncombe County, in which Asheville is located. With the increasing visibility of bears in the area, residents—and wildlife biologists—have questions about the animals. Are these bears larger? Do they have more cubs? Where do they live, and how is the local bear population changing?

A mother bear and her cub inspect a vehicle in Asheville, North Carolina.

BEAR BASICS: WHAT'S FOR DINNER?

- *Bears are omnivores, a type of animal that eats other animals as well as plants.*
- *Their diet varies from acorns, nuts, berries, grasses, plants, grubs, larvae, fish, and fruit to animals such as young deer.*
- *During the fall, acorns are a large part of the bears' diet as they enter* hyperphagia, *a period of time during which they fatten up for the winter denning season. This evolutionary strategy helps them survive the winter, when food is limited or nonexistent.*

For now, residents of Asheville seem tolerant of their neighborhood black bears. Will they be able to coexist with these animals long-term? Do bears and people transmit harmful diseases to one another? What is the potential impact of the rapidly expanding bear population in an urban setting? How do city bears differ from country or rural bears? Four dedicated wildlife biologists are on a search for answers to these questions: PhD candidate Nicholas Gould and Jennifer Strules, wildlife biologists with North Carolina State University; Dr. Christopher DePerno, a professor at North Carolina State University; and Colleen Olfenbuttel, the North Carolina Wildlife Resources Commission's black bear and furbearer biologist. It's Colleen's job—in addition to functioning as the bear study's co–principal investigator—to keep tabs on the population of black bears and of sixteen furbearing animal species in the state. Together, the team is conducting the North Carolina Urban/Suburban Black Bear Study. The five-year field investigation of Asheville's urban/suburban bears will observe how this growing population lives and how it uses Asheville as a resource. The team will interact with bears in their dens and will trap them in large, barrel-shaped culvert traps during the spring and summer months.

The scientists' quest will not take them to the hollows and high country of the surrounding Blue Ridge Mountains, but throughout the city of Asheville, into the neighborhoods and backyards of local residents. These are places that are familiar to me because Asheville is my hometown. Unlike many of my neighbors, however, I have never seen a black

Jennifer Strules, Nick Gould, and Colleen Olfenbuttel arrive at their outdoor "office."

The bear study biologists make their way to the tree den.

bear up close. That's about to change. Nick, Colleen, and Jennifer are heading out into the field and have invited me, along with local wildlife photographer Steve Atkins, to join the bear study so that I can write this book and bring you face-to-face with Asheville's black bears.

〉〉〉〉〈〈〈〈

Twenty feet (6.1 m) from where we're standing, a female black bear is nestled down in a hollowed-out white oak tree for the winter. The bear has great taste in real estate. Her den is in Bill Risdall's backyard, which is inside a large gated housing development. Bill knows what it's like to live with bears. "I see them all the time," he says. "I don't worry about

The bear known as N057 is hidden in this tree. Her den is just below the split between those two large limbs.

being too close. I just have to stay aware and let them have their space." Like Rebecca Dougherty, Bill respects bears as wild animals. He also secures his trash, because the forest around his home is frequented by black bears who have adapted to life near people.

The tree in Bill's yard looks a little worse for the wear to me, but to a black bear in need of a cozy spot to curl up in for the winter, it's ideal because the only entrance to this den is fifteen feet (4.6 m) off the ground. Black bears of Western North Carolina enter dens as early as October and as late as January, then typically emerge from them in March or April. However, contrary to popular belief, bears in this part of the country do not hibernate all winter long, the way bears in colder climates do. If the weather is mild and food is available, male bears and females without cubs may be active during the winter months.

Bill's "neighbor" is already known to the study as N057, the fifty-seventh bear captured and released by the team during the first year of fieldwork in 2014. N057 was captured a second time in a culvert trap in 2015. Over the course of their fieldwork, the biologists have tagged and tracked more than 150 bears.

Every bear in the study receives a unique identification number, a set of ear tags, a *radio collar,* and a corresponding tattoo. Multiple identifiers afford the scientists more than one way to recognize bears in the study, should any single mark fail. The special radio collar includes a *global positioning system (GPS)* and an analog antenna. The antenna signal is used to track the bear when it's close by. The GPS capability allows the scientists to continually track individual bears via satellite across great distances and long periods of time, providing regular locational updates, or data points, that can be

Bill Risdall's mountainside home in Asheville, North Carolina.

plotted on a map on the team's computers throughout the year. Each point shows where a bear is located and how far it has traveled since its last location.

More than eighty property owners have participated in the study so far, and their cooperation is vital to its success. "Private landowners make this work possible," Colleen says. "To study urban bears, we needed to be in urban areas. When we first began this research, we weren't even sure if residents would be willing to let us work with bears near their homes. But the community response has been overwhelmingly positive. If it weren't for people like Bill, we wouldn't have a study."

In fact, one of the study's first big discoveries had to do with humans—not bears: many residents of Asheville are

7

extremely tolerant of the growing bear population. In truth, residents don't have much choice. State wildlife officials will not trap and relocate the bears because it's not a long-term solution. According to Nick, "If we relocated a bear, it's likely that it would return or that another bear would take up residence in its place." The state wants the public to learn to live responsibly with these animals because it's usually a person causing the problem by failing to properly store trash and not being proactive about deterring bear activity.

Although Asheville's bears are tolerant of people, the biologists must exercise extreme care when trapping or working with a bear in a winter den. Their nearly silent approach requires rock-climbing skills as well as experience with archery and rappelling.

All these techniques, combined with plenty of patience, will be helpful in achieving today's goal: making a house call to N057. The team will outfit her with a brand-new GPS radio collar and assess her reproductive status and overall health.

But before we could visit N057's den, we needed to know if she was home. The team located the bear in her den using the radio collar they gave her last year. Once the bear's collar communicated with Jennifer's computer, she knew within a sixty-six-foot (20 m) radius of its signal where the bear was potentially located. "With a portable telemetry receiver tuned to N057's radio-collar frequency, I drove to the area where the collar was sending spatial data from," says Jennifer. As the signal grew stronger (a beeping sound that increases in volume), Jennifer left her vehicle and followed on foot, carrying a portable antenna to its source: the tree den in Bill's backyard.

HIGH-TECH TRACKING

The GPS radio collars used by the bear study biologists.

"Data from GPS radio collars has shown that the bears—especially younger male bears—can roam large expanses of terrain throughout the year," Nick says. "We are learning about the routes, or corridors that they use, how far they travel, and their movements in and around Asheville."

A bear must weigh at least ninety pounds (41 kg) to receive a collar. "Fitting the collar is the most important and sensitive procedure we do," says Nick. "We take great care to try to ensure a good fit that allows for potential growth. It's a delicate process because we do not want the collar to become too tight, but we also do not want the bear to pull the collar off (as they are capable of doing)." The collars also have a few features that help the biologists protect the bears' well-being.

COLLAR	BEAR	LOCATION	TRUTHED/DATE	DATA
21242	N051 ♀	FRENCH BR. RIVER GREENWAY	NO	YES
15269a	N112 ♀	French BR. River/Biltmore	YES-1/24. HEARD 1 CUB	OCC.
15285	N006 ♀	LYNN COVE RD	NO. LANDOWNER HEARD 2 CUBS ~1/11	OCC.
22055	N139 ♀	PEREGRINE LANE	YES-1/18. ∅CUBS	NO
17201	N057 ♀	2015 DEN	YES-1/18. ∅CUBS	NO
16728	N148 ♀	26+40/EXIT 46	YES-1/24. ∅CUBS	NO
17199	N056 ♀	~WINDY GAP	LEFT DEN! 2/12	YES
16724	N131 ♀	BRP + ELK MT HWY	YES-2/11.∅CUBS	YES
17200	N075 ♀	DEXTER DRIVE	YES-2/2.∅CUBS	NO
21240	N061 ♂	BILTMORE/PONY RD	NO	YES
22070	N143 ♀	COUNTRY CLUB RD	YES-2/2.∅CUBS	NO
15266	N146 ♀	AZALEA + HARDESTY LN	NO	YES

Detailed data collection is important to scientists. The bear study biologists manage multiple large databases with various types of computer programs to keep the most accurate and detailed records possible. This whiteboard in their office shows the statuses of some of the study's radio-collared bears.

"First is a small cotton or leather spacer that attaches the collar battery to the belting. This spacer is specifically designed to rot off after some time, and this is important because technology does fail," Nick explains. "So if the collar 'fails' and we can no longer communicate with it (and therefore cannot locate the animal), we know the collar will fall off in a relatively short period (approximately one to two years) and the animal will not wear the collar its entire life."

There are other safety features as well. "The collar is built with a timer-controlled drop-off, which is set at three years," Nick says. "Some of our collars on smaller bears are actually set to drop off this fall after being deployed for only a few months. At three years, the collar will fall off regardless."

One final feature is perhaps the most important. "The collars also have radio-controlled drop-off capability. If for any reason we need to retrieve the collar (e.g., it is malfunctioning, or it appears to be too snug, etc.)," Nick says, "we can get within a specified range of the bear and 'release' the collar. We have successfully deployed this mechanism dozens of times. The majority of those occurrences have been due to some issue regarding collar function."

If a resident reports seeing a bear that seems to be having an issue with a radio collar, the team can easily investigate and remove it. If the bear dies or the collar falls off on its own (or is removed by the bear, which occasionally happens) and records no movement for twelve hours, it emits a special "mortality" signal. The team can use the signal to locate and retrieve either the bear's carcass or the radio collar.

HOW MANY BEARS CAN ASHEVILLE BEAR?

The team uses two terms to judge how well a given area can support its bear population. Biological carrying capacity *refers to the maximum number of individuals of a species that can be sustained in a habitat. In Asheville, that means how many bears can live successfully in the urban environment.*

Social carrying capacity *refers to the number of animals that citizens are willing to tolerate. For some people, one bear in the yard can feel like too many. For others, like Bill, seven, eight, or even ten bears would be acceptable. "The people of Asheville have been very accepting," Chris DePerno says. "Tremendous land-owner support for our study indicates that the city's social carrying capacity is high, and hopefully, people are learning to do the right things to live in close proximity with bears." Removing food sources such as bird feeders and garbage as well as properly storing trash in bear-resistant containers are simple and effective ways to discourage neighborhood bear activity.*

"N057 is not the only bear in the neighborhood," Nick says, pointing in the opposite direction. "We have another female bear, likely unrelated to N057, denning less than a hundred meters [328 feet] away." The second bear, N139, was fitted with a radio collar in 2016. "Ordinarily, it would be odd for these two bears to coexist in such proximity. The fact that they are denning so near to each other is interesting." But N139's presence may underscore the ways in which black bears are adapting to an urban/suburban environment. "Bears are solitary animals," Nick states, "but they will tolerate other bears, especially if food supplies are abundant. Because their home ranges are highly variable, young male bears may have larger home ranges as they look for an area in which to settle. If multiple neighborhood bears find a comfortable home range area that's smaller but offers plenty of food, they will tolerate other bears in the vicinity as long as food remains abundant."

Urban life has made Asheville's bears tolerant of humans and noise, but they still get nervous if people approach their dens. Nick, Colleen, and Jennifer work quietly, relying on hand signals, cell phone text messages, and whispers to communicate. If N057 has cubs inside the den, the scientists want to be careful to avoid distressing her with excess noise before they are in position. Remaining as calm and quiet as possible is essential if the team is going to recapture her successfully. The only sounds are the crunch of leaf litter, a distant train whistle, and the loud chatter of gray squirrels.

Getting close to N057 requires each team member to have the skills of a rock climber. Jennifer will climb the tree and dart the bear today. She grabs a tightly coiled length of rope and a handful of carabiners and fits into the climbing harness she'll need to ascend to the den. That's when I

Nick prepares to shoot the climbing rope over N057's tree.

notice Nick preparing the most surprising piece of gear—a bow and arrow.

Nick, a skilled archer, attaches a climbing rope to an arrow that has a blunt end, and he aims for a fork in the tree's uppermost branches, high above the den opening. He shoots. The rope lands on the other side of the oak, where Colleen secures it as part of Jennifer's climbing apparatus.

Jennifer ties her harness to the rope and nods to the team. It's time to climb. She ascends slowly, hoisting herself up with her hands as she goes.

Ten minutes later she is peeking into the opening of the den. Before firing the dart, she must first determine the bear's position and see if any cubs are present. The team never fires blindly at a bear. Darting a cub by mistake could cause injury or death. The carbon dioxide–powered pistol has a built-in laser sight to show the spot where the dart will enter the thick skin of the bear's shoulder. On the ground,

Jennifer averts her eyes as N057 vacates her den. Bears may interpret direct eye contact as aggression.

Colleen is prepared to fire a second dart into the bear if the animal dashes out of her den.

The biologists are unarmed except for the CO_2 pistols, but they call upon an arsenal of field experience, training, and knowledge about bears and their biology to safely conduct their work. "We respect these animals," Colleen says. "Bears evolved as a prey species with grizzly bears, mountain lions, and wolves. Experience and evolution tell us that this bear will be most interested in escaping as soon as possible."

Once Jennifer is certain that there's no risk of harming any cubs and a suitable target area for the dart is exposed on N057, she raises the barrel of the darting pistol, takes aim, and fires. Jennifer rushes to the left of the den entrance to allow the bear to emerge. N057 is faster than seems possible for such a large animal. In a few seconds she scampers backwards down the tree. Colleen fires a second dart into the bear as she descends, and N057 charges into the woods. Her footfalls are almost silent as her large body disappears into the brush.

The team kicks into high gear. "There's one cub," Jennifer tells the ground crew from her perch in the tree. "Let's get it quickly," says Nick, hoisting a nylon bag up the rope. "We'll need to find N057 ASAP." Jennifer grabs the bag and shimmies feet-first into the den. When she partially emerges moments later, the black bag is wiggling in her hand.

She lowers the cub to Nick while Colleen grabs the

Jennifer prepares to lower N057's cub to the ground after retrieving him from the den.

Colleen uses an antenna and receiver to listen for the signal from N057's radio collar.

receiver and antenna to listen for N057's collar signal. A steady stream of beeps emits from the transmitter. "She's nearby!" Colleen says, handing the receiver to Nick in exchange for the black bag. Jennifer is lowered to the ground and quickly unbuckles her climbing harness. She and Nick snatch up backpacks and the gear they'll need to process N057 once she succumbs to the anesthesia. "We'll text you when we've found her," Jennifer says as she and Nick set off down the steep mountainside in the direction of the bear. Meanwhile, the rest of us are on nursery duty with her tiny cub.

N057's cub.

A mother bear nurses her cubs at a neighborhood carport.

A pair of cubs wrestle near an Asheville home.

BEAR BASICS: ALL IN THE FAMILY

- Bears are solitary animals. After mating, the male bear departs. When cubs are born, the female bear raises them alone.
- Newborn cubs are blind and hairless, weighing approximately one pound (.45 kilograms).
- Bear cubs remain with their mother until they are nearly 1.5 years of age, when they strike out to begin their own independent lives.
- Young bears between the ages of one and two are known as yearlings.

His eyes are blue and have fully opened. "Based on that and his size, he's approximately seven to eight weeks old," Colleen says, handing out blue medical gloves that will protect the cub from germs and human scent. She passes the cub to me with advice to hold him like a small dog. He is easy to handle now, about as large as a six-week-old puppy, but the cub will grow quickly. At this size, it's the only time in his life it will be safe for us to be this close to him in the wild. We are the ones who must be gentle. He's no more dangerous than a kitten, with claws that stick like Velcro to my jacket as he snuggles close to me for warmth. He smells like the forest—earthy, pungent, and wild.

I pass the cub back to Colleen so she can examine him. He squirms against the measuring tape as she places it along his body, then around his midsection, dictating the numbers for me to record on a data sheet. She speaks softly as he growls, grunts, and chuffs. He doesn't like having his paws touched, but he tolerates Colleen's quick inspection of his gums. "His teeth won't emerge for another ten days or so," she says. To check his weight, Colleen places the cub in a pillowcase attached to a handheld scale.

After the measurements are completed, Colleen takes a tissue sample from the corner of the cub's ear and places it in a small vial. The tissue will be used to study the cub's

Colleen measures the cub's paw.

Colleen measures the cub's midsection.

Colleen weighs the cub using a handheld scale and a pillowcase.

genetic makeup. He is too young to be collared or ear-tagged, so Colleen injects a small microchip identifier, called a *PIT (Passive Integrated Transponder) tag,* into the scruff of his neck (like the microchip given to domestic pets by veterinarians). If he's recaptured as an older bear, the team will scan for the microchip and identify him as N057's cub.

"Bear! Hey, bear!" Nick's voice echoes in the distance.

"That's a good sign!" Colleen says to me as she finishes up with the cub. "Sounds like they've found the mother bear." By speaking loudly, Nick is testing N057's reaction to auditory stimuli; if she moves her head in response, the team must quietly wait a few minutes longer for the anesthesia to take effect. Colleen tucks the cub into the pillowcase she will use to carry him down the steep grade to Nick and Jennifer's location. "Okay, little guy," she says to the baby bear. "Let's get you back to your mother."

The downhill hike to N057 is slow and steep. Branches whip at our faces. Knee-deep leaf litter and ankle-twisting logs slow our pace. When we finally arrive, Nick and Jennifer have dug a terrace into the hillside by hand. A small tree limb has been driven into the ground in front of the bear to keep her from rolling downhill during the exam. "We have blindfolded her to protect her eyes from sunlight and debris," Nick says. "Because the bear cannot blink under anesthesia, I administered an eye lubricant to keep them from drying out while she's anesthetized. But keep your voices to a whisper, please. Loud noises could rouse her prematurely, or cause additional stress."

Nick and Jennifer examine N057. A large stick driven into the ground anchors the bear in place on the steep hillside.

A blindfold protects N057's eyes from sunlight and debris.

"We monitor the heart rate and temperature every five to ten minutes," Jennifer explains. "If there are any dramatic spikes or dips, we will end the exam, administer the reversal drug immediately, and continue to monitor her."

"This bear is much bigger than she was last year," Nick says, estimating the bear's weight because the team doesn't have a large portable scale. "She was around one hundred sixty pounds [73 kg] at last capture. She's at least two hundred twenty [100 kg] now."

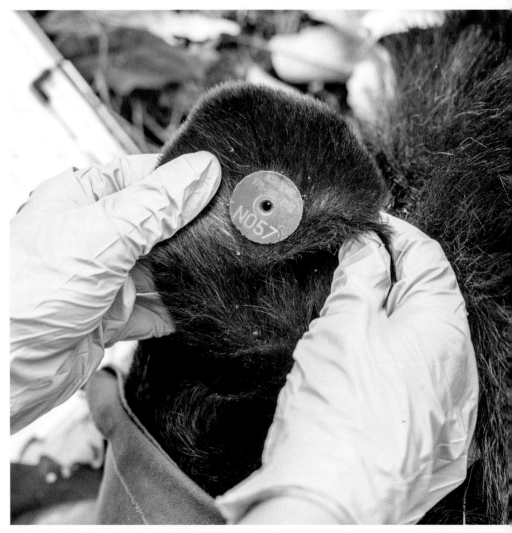

One of N057's ear tags, marked with her identification number.

AMAZING BEAR REPRODUCTION

Female black bears usually begin breeding between the ages of three and eight, depending on food availability and the density of the bear population. Typically, bears breed every other year and exhibit what is known as delayed implantation. *Following fertilization, which occurs during the summer breeding season, the embryo (or blastocyst) does not implant in the uterine wall until the fall (delayed for up to five months). This allows the female bear's body to assess its condition and determine whether or not the bear is fit enough to carry a pregnancy. If her body condition is poor, she will absorb the embryo and not become pregnant, retaining those fat reserves. If a female weighs enough in the fall, she will become pregnant, giving birth approximately two months later. Females in somewhat poor condition may become pregnant, but those pregnancies can fail, or if the cubs are carried to full term, they could die shortly after birth due to lack of milk.*

Do urban bears have more cubs or larger litters? It's too soon to tell. The biologists cannot yet conclude how the overall health of the urban bear population affects the increased numbers of bears, but they're eager to find out more.

I sit down beside N057. Her coat is dense and bristly. As I run my gloved hand along her fur, its color shifts under my touch from black to blue to gray. I hold one of her massive paws. It's heavy! Her claws are long and jagged; the thick footpads are cracked, dry, and callused but also spongy. "That's one reason why it was hard to hear her moving through the forest when she exited her den," Nick says. The thick pads muffle the sound as she walks or runs. Bears' paws are sensitive, so they are careful and deliberate steppers. A bear covering new territory in which another bear's tracks are visible will step into those tracks, likely because it's easier and the ground has already been tested.

A closer look at N057's footpads.

The bear's large wet nostrils flare and contract with each breath as Nick injects the reversal drug that will speed her recovery and help fully wake her in approximately one to three hours.

The unconscious bear and her cub cannot be left out in the open to recover. They would be vulnerable to the elements. But it wouldn't be wise to haul this 220-pound bear back up the steep grade, and it would be impossible to return her to her tree den. The team improvises. We'll reconstruct a den in a nearby stand of mountain laurel shrubs so the mother and cub will be safe until the anesthesia wears off. It will take every spare hand to move the bear, so Steve and I are enlisted to help lighten the load. Bill Risdall, the homeowner, proves his impeccable sense of timing by arriving just when we need someone to babysit the cub. While we transport N057 to her temporary den, Bill carries the cub alongside us.

We each grab one of the canvas sling's nylon handles and lift at Nick's command. We shuffle forward and take periodic breaks to rest our arms and catch our breath. Field science is as physically demanding as it is scientifically challenging. This physical work, like so much of what scientists do, takes patience and a methodical approach. Ten minutes later, the sleeping N057 is braced between two small trees. We've traveled less than fifty feet (15 m) from where we started, but it feels as if we've carried this bear fifteen miles (24 km)!

Everyone lends a hand to carry N057 to the makeshift den.

Bill Risdall with his favorite neighbor, N057's cub.

Nick observes N057 and her cub in the new den.

"We need to make it look and feel like a den," says Nick. "I have no idea if she'll stay here, choose to return to the tree den, or go elsewhere. At least she'll be safe and protected from the elements while she recovers." We snap off branches of mountain laurel and collect large sticks, passing them to Nick and Colleen, who arrange them around the new den. When it's finished, Bill hands the cub to Nick, who places him on the ground for a quick dirt bath, rubbing leaves and dirt all over the cub's body. "It helps mask the scent of humans," Nick says, carefully nestling the cub against his mother's chest. The cub immediately snuggles close for warmth and searches for milk. "The drugs in his mother's system have metabolized quickly and pose no threat to the cub," Nick says. "And this little one won't wander off. His survival instincts tell him to stay close to Mom, where he's safe, warm, and well-fed."

We leave the two bears and gather our gear for the steep hike back to Bill's house. Nick and Jennifer will return to check on N057 and her cub later tonight and again tomorrow morning. We don't know how N057 will take to her new den, but we depart, trusting that mother and cub are safe for the night.

The next day, I receive an email update from Colleen: *"N057 stayed with her cub in the den we built. We were a bit surprised. I guess we did a good job making her a den!"*

Fresh from his "dirt bath," the cub cuddles up to his still-anesthetized mother.

What's the best part of being a field biologist on the bear study? For Colleen, Chris, Nick, and Jennifer, it's about teamwork, community outreach, and the chance for discovery.

Name: *Colleen Olfenbuttel, co–principal investigator, North Carolina Urban/Suburban Black Bear Study; black bear and furbearer biologist, North Carolina Wildlife Resources Commission (NCWRC). It's Colleen's job to know everything she can about black bears and other furbearing animals, such as raccoons, otters, and foxes. She's especially interested in bears' ability to gain weight leading up to hibernation. A bear's diet is more limited in the winter, but Asheville's bears are not deep hibernators, like bears in colder climates. Throughout the winter in Western North Carolina, they may enter and exit their dens to search for food.*

Favorite bear fact: *"Bears gain up to double their body weight in the fall in order to prepare for winter hibernation. If people gained weight the way bears do, they would not only be very unhealthy; they may not survive owing to all the health complications that come with being obese. But bear physiology has evolved so they can gain that much weight and not suffer from diabetes and other health issues. Because of this unique ability, as well as the physiological changes that occur during hibernation (they don't defecate, urinate, eat, etc.), scientists are doing research on what bears can show us about how to treat diabetes, osteoporosis, and muscle loss."*

Name: *Christopher S. DePerno, PhD, co–principal investigator, North Carolina Urban/Suburban Bear Study; professor of fisheries, wildlife, and conservation biology, North Carolina State University.*

Favorite part of the bear study: *"My favorite part of the study is developing applied research questions and working with an excellent team to learn about a species and the ecosystem it inhabits. The answers will allow the NCWRC and other state agencies to incorporate science-based information into their long-term black bear management plans."*

Dr. Christopher DePerno, co–principal investigator, examines a radio-collared bear as part of his fieldwork with the North Carolina Urban/Suburban Bear Study.

Colleen gives the cub a head-to-toe exam.

Field science is a family affair for Nick Gould and his four-year-old daughter, Samantha.

Name: *Nicholas Gould, PhD student, wildlife biologist, North Carolina Urban/Suburban Black Bear Study, North Carolina State University.*

Favorite part of the bear study: *"The overwhelming support for the project by the citizens of Asheville. We connect with homeowners on a daily basis. We hear their personal bear stories, answer their questions about the animals, and watch them when we capture a bear on their property. It has been an incredibly rewarding and educational experience, for both parties. Our work helps to educate and hopefully inspire the next generation to conserve wildlife resources."*

Name: *Jennifer Strules, MS, wildlife biologist, North Carolina Urban/Suburban Black Bear Study, North Carolina State University.*

Favorite part of the bear study: *"We are studying urban black bears. It is very exciting to gather life-history data that may—or may not—vary from bears living in rural areas."*

Not all of Jennifer Strules's work on the bear study involves climbing trees. She also monitors the bears' movements from the office.

CHAPTER TWO
Consequences of Conservation

COLLEEN'S EMAIL UNDERSCORES something important about wildlife conservation: it can be difficult to predict how any wild animal will react when its environment changes. In order to make informed decisions, human beings must carefully observe the ways in which animal populations behave, move, and grow. Yet, historically, human beings have not always made decisions in the best interests of wildlife, especially black bears. In fact, the recent increase in Asheville's urban bear population resulted after their numbers had dropped to historic lows. "In the late 1800s," Colleen says, "the North Carolina black bear population began to decline. Forested areas, which provided habitat for bears, were converted into agricultural croplands." Indigenous people such as the Cherokee—who depended on bears for meat, for fat to season foods, and for hides to make clothing—understood how to use the animals responsibly, but some white settlers were not as conscientious. "They considered bears a threat to crops, resulting in unregulated killing." Bears were often shot outright because they could destroy farmland, particularly corn crops, that people needed for food and income to support their families. Survival outweighed some people's desire to consider more humane alternatives that would have ultimately protected themselves and the bears. "Extensive logging further decimated black bear habitat in the early 1900s," Colleen adds. "The final straw was the introduction of the chestnut blight, which killed off a consistent and abundant source of food for bears. By the mid-1950s, bears were eradicated from the middle of North Carolina, living only in remote areas of the mountains and the coast."

Visitors to North Carolina's Great Smoky Mountains National Park stop to watch a black bear snack at a trash can in 1957. The heavy traffic caused by people stopping on the road due to a bear sighting was known as a "bear jam."

THE DEMISE OF THE MIGHTY AMERICAN CHESTNUT TREE

In 1904, the chestnut blight, a tree-killing fungus known as Cryphonectria parasitica, *was accidentally imported into the United States from Asia. As the infected trees were planted, the disease quickly spread to America's chestnut trees, devastating that tree population. It is estimated that in some parts of the region, before the blight struck Western North Carolina in the 1920s, one in every four hardwood trees was an American chestnut. Mature trees could grow to one hundred feet (30 m), with a trunk diameter of fourteen feet (4.3 m). By 1940, the blight had claimed nearly four billion American chestnut trees nationwide and further devastated North Carolina's black bear population.*

A stand of American chestnut trees ravaged by blight.

Like sharks, black bears are among nature's most misunderstood animals, making them vulnerable to persecution by humans. Movies and advertisements often portray them as deadly predators or cuddly comfort objects, which confuses the public. Bears can be aggressive if provoked, but they are also tolerant, bright, and curious mammals. Part of the problem is that some of their body language is misleading. Nick explains: "One of the most common and false assumptions about bears is how they exhibit aggression. Most people panic if they encounter a bear and it stands up on its hind legs, assuming it's preparing to attack. This stance is actually a posture of curiosity, not aggression. Standing on its hind legs allows the bear to see better, and to get a better look around while using its heightened sense of smell to identify whatever, or whoever, is approaching."

Ironically, affection for the North Carolina black bears also harmed them. These bears charmed local residents and tourists, who fed them by hand. Black bears are sturdy,

Logs cut from forests paved the way for development and opportunity in the Western North Carolina mountains.

Turn-of-the-century sawmill in North Carolina.

Great Smoky Mountains National Park visitors stop to feed a local black bear by hand, 1957.

A man and a young child run from a charging black bear, 1957.

opportunistic animals, able to adjust to new circumstances and environments. Although they are omnivorous, eating mostly plants, berries, grubs, and acorns, the bears' ability to adapt to any nearby food source makes them expert survivors.

Over time, some bears learned to associate human beings with food—and they came looking for it more frequently. Wildlife officials have a saying: "A fed bear is a dead bear," because feeding bears diminishes one of their most important survival instincts—avoiding human beings. Eventually these bears can become comfortable in the human world, learning from experience how to appear tame in order to earn food. Though unprovoked bear attacks were, and remain, statistically rare, bears are wild animals that can be dangerous if provoked. Still, more often than not, it has been the bear who pays the price for this closeness to humans.

BEARS ON THE BRINK

By the early 1970s there were fewer than three thousand bears statewide. Would the iconic American black bear disappear from the state? Concerned wildlife biologists of the NCWRC stepped in to support a bear comeback. The agency changed hunting laws, created approximately eight hundred thousand acres of designated bear sanctuaries, initiated research studies, and began educating the public about bear behavior and biology. The result is one of wildlife conservation's great success stories. But, according to Colleen, with success came questions and complaints.

"In the early 1990s," she says, "the NCWRC started documenting phone calls about human-bear interactions in North Carolina. Tracking the number of human-bear in-

A radio-collared black bear, N015, is released from a trap in a mountaintop neighborhood of Asheville, visible in the distance.

teractions over time can provide scientists with a tool for tracking trends in the bear population. By the mid-1990s, seventy-five to eighty-five percent of those calls came from Western North Carolina, and now a whopping forty-one percent of those calls originate from Buncombe County alone, where Asheville is located." Adult bears do not have natural predators except for humans. With no hunting allowed in the city limits of Asheville, the bears' numbers have been growing steadily over the past four decades. Meanwhile, the human population and land development have increased as well, putting residents in closer proximity to bears. "Every year, more calls flooded our office," says Colleen. "People were curious, excited, or concerned. They wanted to know why there were bears in such a developed area, and if these bears were bigger because of all the artificial food sources."

Colleen had questions of her own. "I wondered if bears living in suburban and urban areas differed from their rural counterparts in activity patterns, reproduction, and movements. Did these bears, who appeared to be very tolerant of humans, leave Asheville to populate the surrounding area, perhaps then causing problems? Were bears from outside the city limits attracted to Asheville due to the abundance of artificial food and absence of hunting? We realized we simply couldn't answer some of the questions about bears living in suburban/urban areas. Hard data was needed to determine how educational outreach efforts, habitat corridors, and hunting strategies could help us minimize human-bear interactions and manage bear numbers in residential developments. In 2014, the North Carolina Urban/Suburban Black Bear Study was born."

NORTH CAROLINA'S BEAR BOOM BY THE NUMBERS

These maps show how the bear population has expanded and concentrated throughout North Carolina. Note that most of the bears live in the extreme western and eastern parts of the state.

North Carolina bear population growth between 1970 and 2014

1970: 1,500–3,000

2001: 10,000–13,000

2010: 14,000–17,000

2014: 15,500–19,000

This color-coded map shows the gradual expansion of the black bear population in North Carolina from 1971 to 2010.

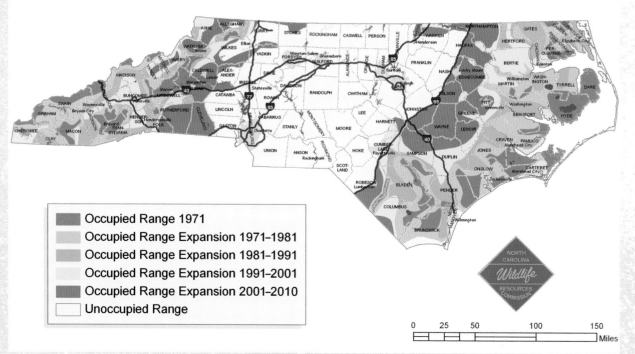

North Carolina
Black Bear Occupied Range Expansion
1971–2010

Occupied Range 1971
Occupied Range Expansion 1971–1981
Occupied Range Expansion 1981–1991
Occupied Range Expansion 1991–2001
Occupied Range Expansion 2001–2010
Unoccupied Range

NORTH CAROLINA *Wildlife* RESOURCES COMMISSION

0   25   50   100   150   Miles

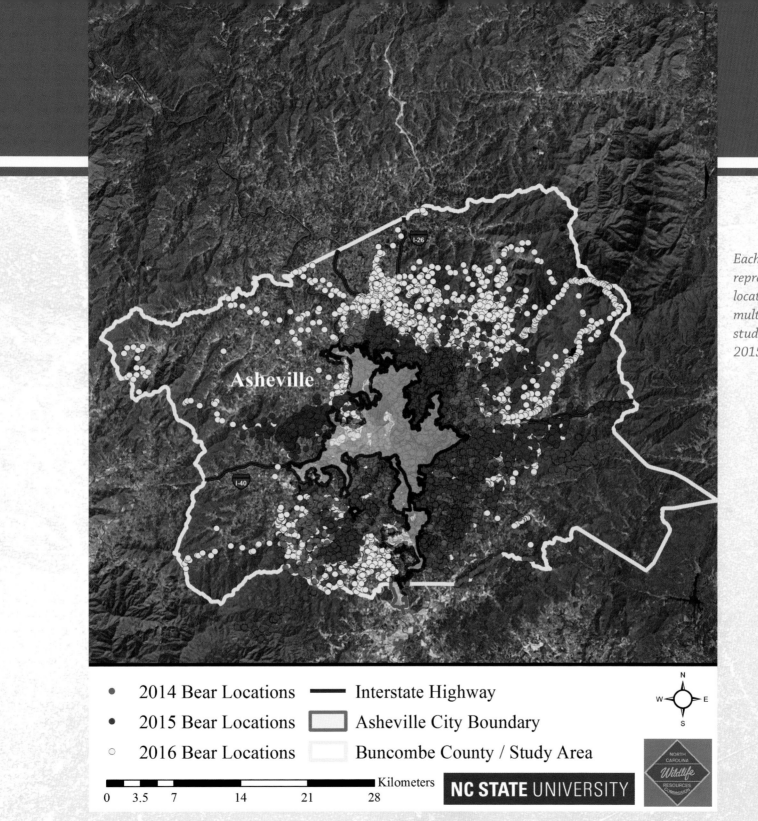

Each colored circle represents a single location point for multiple bears in the study, by year (2014, 2015, 2016).

Asheville

I-26

I-40

- 2014 Bear Locations
- 2015 Bear Locations
- 2016 Bear Locations

Interstate Highway

Asheville City Boundary

Buncombe County / Study Area

Kilometers

0   3.5   7   14   21   28

NC STATE UNIVERSITY

NORTH CAROLINA Wildlife RESOURCES COMMISSION

The bear study is the first of its kind in the southeastern United States, and it seeks to answer the following questions:

1. How do bears survive (or fail to survive) in urban areas like Asheville? What are their survival rates in an urban/suburban habitat? When are they most active? Are the reported sightings or interactions between people and bears the result of a few bears or lots of bears?
2. How do bears move in and around urban and suburban areas? Do they spend their whole lives within city limits, or just a portion of their lives, and how does this affect their survival rate? How do bears use these areas as their home ranges annually and seasonally?
3. What are the characteristics of den sites? Do urban bears den or hibernate in winter, and if so, where and for how long? Do bears use "natural" corridors to move through the urban/suburban landscape, and are these urban/suburban bears vulnerable to harvest (legalized hunting) in the fall?
4. How does living in urban areas affect litter sizes, den sites, and the timing of when black bears enter and emerge from their winter dens?

This information will help wildlife managers better understand a number of factors: what attracts bears to urban/suburban environments, whether Asheville is serving as a source or a sink for the surrounding bear population, which natural corridors could be conserved in order to reduce the proximity of people and bears, and if bears living in or near Asheville are susceptible to harvest. Bear study data will provide them with new information to educate residents on how to prevent future human-bear interactions.

The biologists will track hundreds of black bears between 2014 and 2018, monitoring each bear for a period of at least six months across several years. The goal is to follow approximately forty bears per year. The team will gather data on bears in their dens, capture them in culvert traps throughout Asheville, and track their movements. Their results could help wildlife officials make more informed, science-based wildlife management decisions. Teaching people how to coexist with wildlife is another desired outcome, and it begins with educating the public. When residents report bears on their property, the team strives to turn those reports into opportunities for scientific observation.

A resident once called to report that seventeen bears were feasting on acorns that had fallen from three mature white oak trees in her yard. "Because we had previously trapped nearby," Nick says, "I knew there were quite a few bears in the area. It was also the second-best mast year on record since 1983. [*Mast* refers to fruit of the forest, such as acorns, other nuts, and berries.] Bears were especially interested in places where white oak trees were dropping huge quantities of acorns—but seventeen bears? I was impressed." The resident's report proved correct and underscored something that has been known about bears in general for a long time: large numbers of bears tolerate one another as long as there is plenty of food to go around.

On another occasion, a concerned citizen called the NCWRC to report a group of four large bears in his yard. The bears, a mother and her three yearlings, were familiar to the study because the mother had been captured and released the previous year, when her young were still cubs. A typical yearling weighs between 50 and 80 pounds (23–36 kg), but the three brothers weighed in at 183, 206, and 208 pounds

Steve Atkins spotted this group of bears—one of whom is wearing a radio collar—on his way to work after our participation in the bear study concluded.

35

MARK OF THE BEAR

Tree marking by male black bears is common, especially during the summer mating season. They stand on their hind legs and scratch the trees with their claws and sometimes their teeth. It is uncertain whether bears mark trees to convey social information to other bears, though many researchers suspect it's a dominance display— a way for one bear to let other bears in the area know they are in the neighborhood and how big they are. But they don't always need a tree to make their mark. Manmade structures such as utility poles, footbridges, and even outbuildings may also be scratched or chewed. Bears also rub their backs against trees or other objects to relieve irritation caused by parasites (fleas, ticks) and to loosen their thick winter coats as they shed during summer. If a bear finds a good scratching tree, it may be used repeatedly for several years.

SIZING UP NORTH CAROLINA'S BEARS

The average size of an American black bear is 5 to 6 feet (1.6–1.8 m) long and approximately 2 to 3 feet (61–91 cm) tall. They typically weigh from 200 to 700 pounds (91–318 kg). The current world record for the largest black bear ever documented belongs to a bear found in North Carolina. The 880-pound (399-kg) bear was discovered in the coastal region of the state, living off hog carcasses from a nearby farm.

(83, 93, and 94 kg)—four times larger than average for their age! The report led the team to an interesting research question: Are Asheville's bears larger than rural bears? By turning reports of bear sightings into opportunities to do science, the team learns more about the ecology of black bears in urban areas and at the same time helps residents understand how to coexist with them. "We can't control how many acorns will fall in a given year, but we can make neighborhoods less bear-friendly by removing accidental food sources. If the food source is removed," says Colleen, "bears will go elsewhere to eat." Discouraging one bear is not enough, though. It would take entire communities collectively discouraging bear activity on a large scale to notice any reduction in the urban bear sightings and reports in Asheville. Thanks to the bear study biologists and the city's curious and observant citizen scientists, however, residents are learning how to live near bears while making their neighborhoods less bear-friendly.

A captured bear waits inside a culvert trap.

FREE-RANGE BEARS

Firsthand observations matter, but the detailed radio collar data reveals other valuable information: when, where, and how far bears in the study wander in their home ranges. "Right now we have logged a total of 578,000 locations for bears in our study," Nick says. "Before the addition of GPS to the radio collar, that quantity of data would have taken decades to record." Collar data shows that bears differ widely in their movements. While some choose a specific area and stay there, other bears (typically the younger males) like to roam a greater range, traveling twenty to thirty miles (32–48 km) in search of food, shelter, and mates. "Some of them leave the city limits and wander more than a hundred miles [161 km]," Nick says. "One bear left Asheville and traveled over one hundred and sixty miles [257 km] before returning. That really surprised us." Tracking data from the collars suggests that the bears crisscross the city in every direction. Some bears are captured in the city and remain there, while others leave, preferring remote areas. Life for these "country bears" is potentially more dangerous. Unlike bears within the city limits of Asheville, they are more vulnerable to hunting during the annual legal bear harvest.

Not everyone believes in hunting. It's up to individuals to decide for themselves, but the reality is that many bear populations near cities are managed through legal harvests. "It was hunters who first noticed the decline in North Carolina's black bears and sounded the alarm," Colleen says. "Their observations and cooperation led to a change in hunting laws that helped to reestablish the population. A portion of the money raised from the sale of hunting licenses helps fund the state's bear management program. It also supports research to educate the public about wild animal safety and behavior (including bears), as well as natural habitat conservation."

The biologists need to know if Asheville's urban bears are more or less susceptible to hunting if they leave the city. Therefore, tagged and collared bears in the study are not protected during hunting season. However, it is illegal to harvest a female with cubs, or a bear under seventy-five pounds (34 kg). "Tagged bears can be legally harvested," Colleen says, "and accurate mortality data is important to our results. We encourage hunters to notify us if they harvest a bear that is tagged or wearing one of our collars. To understand the population dynamics of these suburban/urban bears, we need to know about all causes of mortality. Were they legally harvested? Did they die of natural causes? Did a vehicle hit them? To exempt bears because they are participating in the study would create a huge bias in our results. None of our conclusions would be reliable."

It's one of the most challenging parts of the scientists' job—distancing themselves from their subjects. While Colleen, Nick, Chris, and Jennifer are passionate about working with wildlife, their job as scientists requires that they must separate their feelings from their desire to know the facts. "It can be hard, especially when a female or a cub is hit by a car," Colleen says. "This job isn't for everyone."

CONSERVATION COMPLICATIONS

Managing an entire population of animals is a balancing act, particularly when those animals are large, potentially dangerous, and living in close proximity to people. Citizens rely on state agencies such as the NCWRC to spread the word about personal responsibility and the importance of safety when living near wildlife. While disagreements arise about solutions, Asheville's bear numbers are increasing. It's a complex situation that is as much about people as it is about the bears. However, by relying on scientists to gather data before making decisions or rushing to snap judgments, we can better understand our environment. It can be uncomfortable to look at all sides of an issue you feel strongly about, especially when animals are involved. But when it comes to long-term conservation and wildlife population management, we must be willing to ask tough questions about what is safe, realistic, and necessary in order to balance habitats shared by all living things.

This wild black bear wandered through someone's yard, just outside Asheville.

A mother bear and her curious cub inspect a pickup truck.

Planning for the future of Asheville's bears means finding homeowners who are willing to allow the scientists to park a bear trap on their property. It seems like a lot to ask, but, as with all things related to the bear study, residents have been eager to help. From the beginning, community outreach was key, and locating trap sites was one of the first challenges, Nick says. "I described the goals of the study, how we would capture and handle the bears on-site, and how the work depended on community involvement. The response was overwhelming. Once people understood that we wouldn't be attracting new bears to their property, just trapping and collaring the ones already in the area, and that we would be on-site to regularly monitor the traps, they were even more enthusiastic!" Almost overnight, the team began appearing on local television and radio and in the newspapers. More people wanted bear traps in their backyards, including some local businesses. Before long, Nick and Jennifer were turning people away and at the same time staying busy conducting follow-ups on the bears they had already trapped and reporting back to residents on their neighborhood's bear activity. "'How's *my* bear doing?' people would ask," Nick says. "It was satisfying to see them investing in their neighborhood's wildlife in ways they never expected—in ways *we* never expected, frankly. It has also become one of the best parts of our job."

The team has been hard at work addressing civic groups, schools, and homeowner associations, as well as chatting with curious residents who visit the study's Facebook page. Each interaction is a chance to inform people about living responsibly with black bears and to replace fear with facts. With every capture, the team is chipping away at decades-old assumptions about bears, as residents see the science for themselves and get close to the animals at the safest place they know—their homes. By directly involving communities in wildlife research, the team shows people through personal experience that life among bears can be wondrous, enjoyable, and relatively safe, despite their growing numbers in Asheville.

BIRTH CONTROL FOR BEARS?

Birth control for bears, also known as *immunocontraception,* is one proposed solution to slow urban bear population growth. However, according to Dr. Chris DePerno, birth control is neither an effective nor a feasible way to regulate the number of bears in Asheville. "As wildlife biologists, we manage populations, not individuals. To see a population-level response from immunocontraception, you would have to treat approximately seventy percent of the females in the population. That level of treatment is necessary just to *stabilize* their numbers. To see a *reduction* in those numbers, you would have to go above and beyond that seventy percent mark. Sometimes the animals must be treated with multiple doses, multiple times over multiple years—and these are animals that live in the wild. They are not in an enclosed setting or a zoo." It's also not financially feasible, Chris says. "Immunocontraception would cost thousands of dollars per individual bear, not to mention the costs for personnel, time, equipment, and vehicles." There is also concern about how long-term exposure to birth control drugs would affect the behavior of bears. With limited funding in the state's budget, it is an expensive and high-risk strategy, with no guarantee of success.

This is the challenge of managing wildlife populations in any setting, not just in urban areas: there are no guarantees. The bear study biologists can evaluate the reproduction of urban bears, study their ecology, and educate residents on how to live responsibly with them. However, it remains to be seen whether these urban bears will be welcome if the animals' numbers continue to rise. The future is uncertain, but data from the bear study could help not just Asheville—other cities around the United States—learn to manage their own urban animal populations, because the story unfolding in North Carolina is not an isolated case. In cities and countries around the globe, urban areas are expanding. Heavily populated cities and neighborhoods can attract nature's most capable survivors and, sometimes, its deadliest predators. From Boston to Berlin and Honolulu to Mumbai, many parts of the world are facing a new and wilder frontier.

One of Mumbai's "ghost leopards" prowls through a
neighborhood inside Sanjay Gandhi National Park.

CHAPTER THREE
A World Going Wild

HUMAN INTERVENTION CHANGES the natural world. The United Nations projects that the human population will reach 11.2 billion by the year 2100. As our population expands, we have to consider the impact on wildlife whose habitats could be compromised or destroyed altogether. Will they die off, or will they adapt, as Asheville's black bears have, learning to live in close proximity to people? In fact, there are animals already adapting to various types of human intervention around the world. In some cases, the results are unexpected and dangerous—creating big changes in living conditions as people and wildlife share closer quarters in evolving urban and suburban landscapes.

LIFE WITH LEOPARDS

"Living ghosts" haunt the city of Mumbai. That's what the local Mumbaikars call them, but the thirty-five flesh-and-blood leopards (*Panthera pardus*) that make their home in this crowded city are real. To the twenty million people who live in Mumbai, the wealthiest and most densely populated city in India, the urban leopards are inconvenient neighbors at best. At worst, they are efficient killers of small prey, and sometimes of people, with 176 attacks on humans recorded between 1991 and 2013.

Sanjay Gandhi National Park (SGNP) is in the city of Mumbai and is the largest urban tropical forest in the world. Bordered by eleven sprawling neighborhoods, the lush forest covers forty square miles (104 square km) of the city, equivalent to thirty times the area of New York City's Central Park. Over 1,000 species of plants and animals are found here, including two dozen types of mammals, 274 species of birds, 170 species of butterflies, a variety of reptiles and amphibians—and nearly 300,000 Mumbaikars who live in and around the park.

For centuries the forest has thrived as this bustling world center has grown up around it. But the relationship between the park's leopards and its people has always been a delicate balancing act. Removing the leopards was once a popular management strategy, but it was short-lived and proved ineffective. Relocating leopards from their human-shared territory only created room for new leopards. These newcomers, unaccustomed to life among people, were frightened and unfamiliar with this foreign territory, resulting in increased attacks on humans.

In recent years Mumbaikars have adopted an alternative strategy: coexisting with the big cats, accepting them as a fact of life. Residents line their roofs with tin to discourage leaping leopards from approaching their homes, and people have begun educating themselves about leopard behavior. Community workshops teach basic safety rules, such as keeping children and pets indoors at night when the animals prowl the quiet streets and trash dumps in search of food. This commonsense approach has made leopard attacks on people relatively infrequent. By working with the animals' nature instead of against it, the city of Mumbai protects its citizens and strikes a balance between human and animal populations.

A NEW TOP DOG

Unlike Mumbai's leopards, one of North America's top predators is an urban animal that numbers in the millions. The eastern coyote (*Canis latrans*) appeared around 1919, when a western coyote first interbred with a wolf in the Canadian wilderness. Although it is unusual for species to interbreed, low availability of food and mates, as well as persecution by humans, made it difficult for the wolf population to survive. When healthy western coyotes migrated to the area, the wolves bred with them to reinvigorate the wolf population. The result was a new type of coyote, a hybrid animal, weighing approximately fifty-five pounds (25 kg) more than pure western coyotes, with longer legs, a larger jaw, smaller ears, and a bushier tail. The animal has been nicknamed "coywolf." However, Dr. Roland Kays of North Carolina State University, who has studied these animals extensively, says that the term is inaccurate. "Over time, the eastern coyote interbred with dogs, too." Today's eastern coyote is part wolf, part coyote, and part dog. But this is not an animal you would want as a pet. It is a strong *apex predator,* an animal not preyed upon by other animals. Although its primary food source is rodents and other small mammals, the combination of wolf and coyote DNA makes it capable of taking down full-grown deer.

How did the eastern coyote spread across the United States and into such metropolitan areas as Chicago and New York? It's an accomplished traveler. Rather than struggling to forge new routes from the wilderness to cities in search of food, it follows in our tracks—our railroad tracks, that is—to migrate. Upon arriving in unfamiliar territory, the

An eastern coyote searches for prey. While these animals are at home in urban/suburban areas, it is rare to see them in cities. They are adept at staying hidden from view.

A feral chicken checks out the waves near Hawaii's famous coast.

eastern coyote does what it does best: hunt. The genetic combination of wolf and coyote makes it easy for the animal to prey on deer, rodents, and other small mammals, helping to balance the ecosystem. But the dog genes are what make the eastern coyote a true urban animal; it is comfortable around people, feeling right at home in neighborhoods and noisy cities. In fact, in the relatively short natural history of the eastern coyote, it has spread to nearly all fifty states and as far south as Mexico. These smart city slickers have been observed stopping to look both ways before crossing a busy street or a highway.

FREE BIRDS

Why did the chicken cross the road? To get to the beach, of course! Tourists, it seems, aren't the only ones flocking to the Aloha State. Thousands of feral chickens (*Gallus gallus domesticus*) roam these islands, basking on Hawaii's pristine sands and strutting across its boardwalks. "They're absolutely everywhere," says Eben J. Gering, an evolutionary biologist at Michigan State University who has been studying these truly free-range birds. "They seem to be living a whole diversity of lifestyles, from eating garbage and cat food to being fed by tourists at the beach."

Like other urban and suburban animals, Hawaii's feral chickens have reached impressive numbers; there are as many as twenty thousand on the island of Oahu alone. The birds have enjoyed a foothold here for some eight hundred years. Centuries before James Cook explored the volcanic islands in 1778, the ancestors of Hawaii's modern-day chickens arrived with its first explorers, the Polynesians. The expert seafaring voyagers carried chickens with them wherever they sailed.

What's the trouble with so many chickens? If you've ever heard a rooster crow, you get the idea. The tens of thousands of these birds in Hawaii are making themselves heard in places inhabited by people. Their loud vocalizations go on for hours, from late at night until first light, leaving angry, sleep-deprived people searching for a solution. That's where it gets complicated. Some of these birds are red jungle fowl (*Gallus gallus*), a chicken-like species that is protected by the state. On the other hand, "free-roaming chickens" (those found in urban areas) are *not* protected. Yet it is almost impossible for the average person to tell the difference. Some Hawaiian cities have adopted a controversial policy of capturing and euthanizing "nuisance" chickens, while other municipalities opt to make them available to Hawaiians as an organic, free-range food source.

Still, despite the noise and political squawking about how to control them, Hawaii's feral chickens provide a valuable public service by consuming large quantities of insects. By eating everything from roaches and wood-destroying termites to venomous scorpions and stinging seven-inch (8-cm)-long centipedes, these controversial "birds of paradise" help balance the island ecology.

Feral chickens are found on each of Hawaii's eight main islands. The largest population of birds lives on Kauai.

URBAN TURKEY TAKEOVER

Honolulu isn't the only city experiencing an urban poultry uprising. Boston has gone to the birds too—to the wild turkeys (*Meleagris gallopavo*), to be exact. They stroll down the streets of the historic city, from Harvard Yard to Fenway Park. When they aren't stopping traffic, the turkeys are stopping Bostonians in their tracks. No one wants to tussle with these bold and often aggressive birds that, according to Massachusetts wildlife officials, can view people as "subordinate."

It hasn't always been this way. When settlers first arrived at Plymouth Rock, they were delighted by the abundance of turkeys in New England, hunting them for food and sport. However, by the 1900s, the tenacious turkey had been hunted into near extinction.

As the environmental movement began to take root in the late 1960s and early 1970s, biologists hoped to revive the wild turkey population in the northeastern United States. In 1972 they trapped thirty-seven wild turkeys in New York and released them into the forests of Massachusetts.

As the well-fed birds evolved, they grew stronger and better able to tolerate New England's harsh winters. Eventually they migrated into the lush green spaces of neighborhoods and city parks, doing their part to gobble up insect pests that bother people.

Now, after decades of urban living, the wild turkey population continues to grow unchecked because the species is protected by law. It's up to residents to create a humane barrier between themselves and wildlife where a natural one no longer exists. Massachusetts wildlife officials suggest making loud noises or spraying the turkeys with garden hoses, but they also urge caution. During the breeding season, the brazen birds have been known to attack people, pets, and even city buses!

TIPS FOR DEALING WITH URBAN TURKEYS

No Treats for Turkeys
Direct or indirect feeding teaches urban turkeys to appear tame to get food. Clean up spilled birdseed. Never hand feed wild turkeys. The desire for food can make them aggressive, especially during breeding season.

Take Charge
Turkeys are bold and brave. If you feel threatened by a bossy bird, discourage it with loud noises or spray from a water hose.

Take Cover
Turkeys can mistake their own reflection or a shiny object for an enemy and may attack it, damaging property. If a turkey takes to tapping on shiny car fenders, mirrors, or glass doors, cover or remove the object of its aggression.

Guard Your Garden
Gardens are filled with grubs and other goodies wild turkeys like to eat. Netting or wire fencing keeps them out of the vegetables and out of your way.

A trio of urban turkeys files into a backyard near Brookline, Massachusetts.

SHAKESPEARE'S STUBBORN STARLINGS

If urban wild turkeys rule Boston's city streets, the European —or common—starling (*Sturnus vulgaris*) commands the skies over North America. As accomplished aerial artists, these birds fly in large, shape-shifting flocks called *murmurations*. How starlings communicate to perform their in-flight bird ballet remains a mystery to scientists. What is clear, however, is that despite the iridescent-feathered beauty of these sturdy, short-tailed birds, they are considered urban pests in the United States. So who's to blame for the European starling invasion? Would you believe it's William Shakespeare?

The story of the European starling in the United States begins with devoted Shakespeare fans. In the late nineteenth century, a group called the American Acclimatization Society hoped to bring to the United States all six hundred species of birds mentioned in Shakespeare's plays. Between 1890 and 1891 the society released approximately one hundred starlings in New York City's Central Park. By the 1950s the Bard's birds were abundant from New York to California and southward, all the way to Mexico. Today there are at least two hundred million starlings in North America, and they have been classified as an *invasive species*, a non-native species whose introduction can harm the ecosystem. Like other successful urban animal populations, starlings flock to cities, where food is abundant. Well-manicured public parks and green spaces teem with worms and insects, staples of the starlings' diet. They are fast-breeding, fast-moving, adaptive birds who nest in city buildings, wherever they can find a nook or cranny.

Starlings cause widespread damage in cities, though: their highly acidic excrement eats through metal and concrete, resulting in widespread property damage. Large flocks of the birds produce fecal waste in such high quantities that sidewalks become impassable. And they wreak havoc on agriculture. In Washington State alone, they were responsible for $9 million in damages to agricultural operations over five years. Nationwide, they have caused an $800 million loss in agricultural damages. In Indianapolis, Indiana, as flocks of forty thousand of the aggressive birds arrive in the city nightly, they must be shooed away by city workers armed with non-lethal lasers and pyrotechnic explosions. Starling strikes have caused catastrophic engine failure in aircraft as well. In 1960, a civilian plane crashed in Boston, killing sixty-two people. In 1996, a military cargo plane crashed in the Netherlands, killing thirty-four. Starlings can also pose a severe risk to human health, carrying a disease called *histoplasmosis,* which can be fatal.

Their reputation is understandably bad, but perhaps Shakespeare would agree that the starlings' tale is a tragic one. These beautiful, quirky little songbirds were never supposed to be here in the first place.

A European starling.

A murmuration, or a flock of starlings, takes the shape of an elephant.

THE WILD BOARS OF BERLIN

The starling invasion began with a love of literature, but Berlin's wild boar (*Sus scrofa*) boom is the result of politics and city planning. Berlin prides itself on being a "green city." Its 3.5 million residents enjoy a multitude of natural spaces that include parks and forested areas. However, thoughtful landscape design and a progressive attitude toward conservation have also made the city appealing to large number of urban boars. Thousands of the portly, fur-covered pigs, their hungry young in tow, have infiltrated Berlin's neighborhoods. The boars have long, potentially deadly tusks and can weigh up to four hundred pounds (181 kg). They troll the city in groups of twenty or more, causing traffic accidents, rooting up greenways, and occasionally charging and killing people. Urban boars are like urban black bears: omnivores that prefer the acorns, grasses, and insect larvae found in abundance in Berlin's city parks and neighborhoods, where their only natural predators are human beings. Their population is controlled by regulated harvests within the city limits, but one study reported that at least 25 percent of Berliners believe that the boars have the right to share their space. Others have argued for birth control to regulate boar numbers. However, as with Asheville's urban bears, a birth control protocol would be difficult to carry out, with no guarantee of success.

Opinions about the boars are divided, but ironically, it was a desire to unite Berlin that triggered the boar boom in the first place. Between 1961 and 1989 Berlin was divided by a large wall that separated Communist-held East Berlin from West Berlin. Communism collapsed in Central and Eastern Europe in 1989, and by 1992 the Berlin Wall had been completely demolished—and so had the barrier between West Berlin and a large population of East Berlin's wild boars. The wall came down, and the boars poured in, forever changing the city's relationship with wildlife.

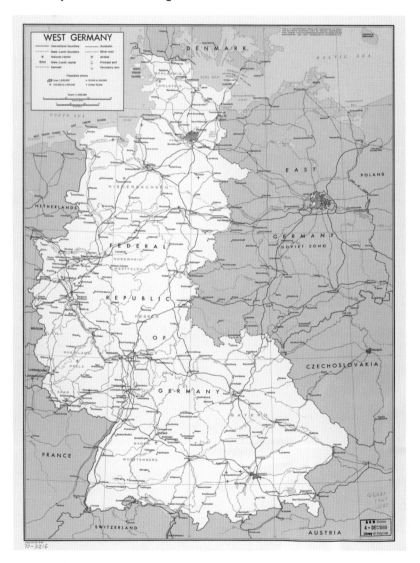

This map, drawn in 1969, depicts the separation of East and West Germany. Erected in 1961, the Berlin Wall stood between eleven and thirteen feet tall, spanning 100 miles. It was torn down in 1990.

A family of wild boars in Berlin roots for grubs and insects next to a busy street.

THE GREAT CAPYBARA ESCAPE

The destruction of a wall may have given rise to Berlin's wild boar population, but erecting a fence is one possible way to prevent an emerging animal population from taking hold of cities in northern Florida. In 1995, five capybaras (*Hydrochoerus hydrochaeris*) escaped from a wildlife facility near Gainesville. At one hundred pounds (45 kg) and around four feet (1.2 m) tall, the capybara is the largest rodent on earth. Native to South America, capybaras thrive in warm, tropical climates and live in groups near areas with plenty of water and heavy vegetation. They are also reliable breeders, producing four to eight pups per litter. It's the capybara's ability to reproduce so successfully that concerns Dr. Elizabeth Congdon, assistant professor of biology at Bethune-Cookman University in Daytona Beach, Florida. "Sightings of the animals in northern Florida suggest that they could still be breeding," she says, "and it's possible that the five escaped animals may have created a breeding population of at least fifty-five, now roaming northern Florida. They might be able to make a go of it in the United States." For now, the capybaras have not established themselves as an urban population in Florida, but in their native South America, they are, and they destroy valuable corn and sugar cane crops. Could they pose a future agricultural threat to the United States if their numbers continue to grow? Might capybaras one day become a new urban/suburban animal here in the States?

Dr. Congdon believes it's a possibility, as capybaras have no natural predators in the area to keep their numbers in check. For now the goal is to contain the animals, either with fencing or more extreme control measures such as the relocation of large males or breeding females. "It's a fine line for those of us studying these animals," says Dr. Congdon. "I love them . . . They are my favorite animal on the planet, but at the same time, it may be necessary to remove them from here."

>>><<<

We cannot remove or destroy every animal that claims an urban space. Our ability to adapt—and, in some cases, survive—depends on our willingness to share the world with wildlife in innovative ways. Science may be the only answer to this new call of the wild.

Capybaras are highly social animals, quite tolerant of other species. Here, a yellow-headed caracara bird sits on a capybara's head.

CHAPTER FOUR
"What a Bear!"

ON WEDNESDAY, MAY 2, I get the call I've been waiting for. It has been two months since our visit with N057 and her cub at their tree den. "Jennifer has captured a small bear in one of our traps in East Asheville," Nick Gould says. "You and Steve should get there ASAP. She won't delay processing that bear any longer than she has to."

The photographer, Steve Atkins, is on a school field trip with his kids, and he brings the class along to see the bear for themselves.

Jennifer discovered this new bear on her daily inspection of the culvert traps deployed throughout Asheville. The safe enclosures secure the animal until the biologists arrive during their twice-daily inspections or if the property owner notifies the team of a capture. Each trap is baited with day-old doughnuts and other pastries from a local grocery store. Bears are opportunistic, drawn to any food source they detect. As long as it's edible, they may eat it, especially sweet foods. Each trap has a trigger with an attached "bait canister" that holds the pastries. To reach the bait, the bear must step all the way inside the trap and pull the trigger with the bait attached to it, causing the door to shut.

Jennifer Strules prepares to examine a trapped black bear in Asheville, North Carolina.

The teacher, Kathryn Taylor, and students from Montessori Elementary School of Asheville observe the bear biologists in action.

It's spring now, and when the bear study concludes in late August, the traps will be removed to protect any curious animals from accidental capture. While trapping, the team checks every twelve hours for bears, or any other occupants that might wander in, such as raccoons, opossum, and foxes.

The trap is empty when we arrive, and there's a small anesthetized male bear resting comfortably on a red tarp. We watch quietly as the team prepares to examine him. "We were surprised to learn this bear is male," Jennifer says, "because he's the size of a young female, only one hundred and nine pounds [49 kg]." Both wrists of his front paws appear to be disfigured, perhaps due to an injury at some point in his life, but there is no way to identify the cause. For this reason, the bear will not be fitted with a radio collar.

Bears like human food, especially sugary sweets. This bear study trap is baited with cupcakes and doughnuts. The interior of the trap has also been smeared with frosting.

Steve's son, Mason Atkins, checks out the trap that caught N157.

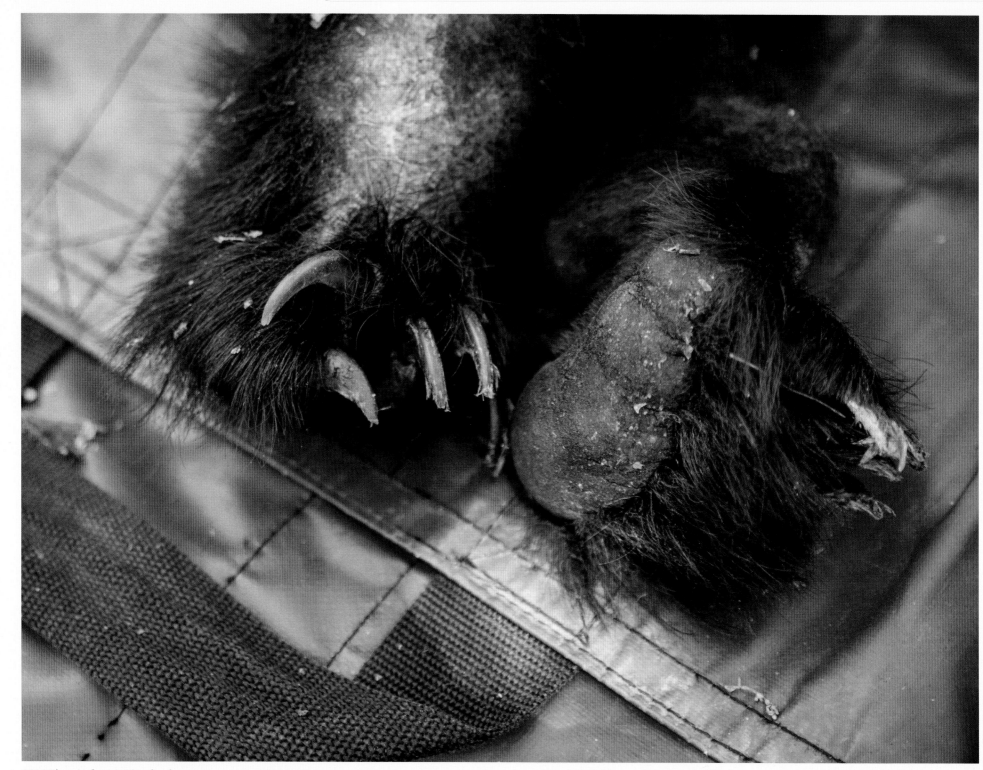

N157's misshapen forelimbs.

The team's first order of business is identification. Each new bear must be cataloged, so he is assigned a study number, N157. He is the 157th bear captured by the team. "We are giving him the same numeric identifiers that all bears in the study receive," Jennifer explains. "A set of ear tags, a small tattoo on the inside of his upper lip that matches his ear tag number, and a PIT tag." Due to his small size for a male, he won't be fitted with a radio collar, so the biologists won't be able to track N157 remotely. But if they recapture him in the future, they will be able to identify him.

We watch as Jennifer gently examines the bear's teeth. "He may be a bit older than a yearling, based on how worn the teeth are," she says.

"Does the bear feel what you're doing to him?" Steve's eight-year-old daughter, Lyla, asks as an ear tag is attached.

"Not at all," says Jennifer. "They don't feel anything, because we put them to sleep first. They wouldn't allow us to examine them if they were awake."

Hair and blood samples are taken next. "Hair samples are for genetic testing," Jennifer says. "We might learn which family the bear belongs to and who his parents are." N157's genetic test might also offer clues about where he came from, or whether he's related to other bears already cataloged in the study. "The blood samples tell us if the bear carries any diseases. Since these animals live in urban areas, we would like to know if they are carriers of diseases that could harm people, or if these bears are contracting human diseases."

Jennifer injects N157 with an antibiotic to help protect him from infection and gives him pain medication to reduce any discomfort caused by these procedures. She rechecks the bear's heart rate and temperature before measuring his

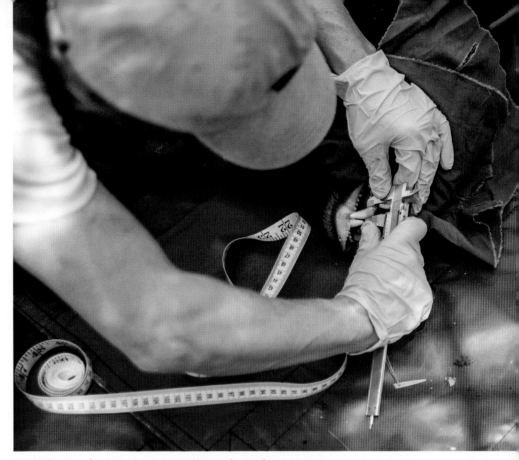

Jennifer Strules measures one of N157's teeth.

body, paws, and head. His front paws are bent at an awkward angle due to his suspected injuries. They have healed, but improperly, so it makes them difficult to measure. When a person breaks a limb, the doctor sets the broken bone so that it heals in the correct position. N157 had to do the best he could on his own. I wondered if his small size was related to his misshapen paws. But Jennifer cautions me against jumping to conclusions. We don't know this bear's history. We can't be sure whether his injuries affected his ability to gain weight or find food. It's easy to make connections that seem logical but aren't necessarily true. Scientists don't have the luxury of assumptions. They report only what they can prove.

Steve's daughter, Lyla Atkins, and N157.

Bodie (left) and Mason try on a GPS radio collar.

We say goodbye to N157 as Jennifer administers the reversal drug, and the team returns him to the trap to safeguard his recovery for the next few hours. When the bear is awake and able to move on his own, Jennifer will climb on top of the trap and open the door to release him.

For safety reasons, and to reduce N157's stress level, we won't be able to observe when he is released, so the students take turns touching his thick fur a final time before we leave. It's one thing to spot a bear in your neighborhood, but being this close is a once-in-a-lifetime experience.

We are all concerned about the bear, given his injuries, and we are eager to hear how the release concluded. The next day, I receive an email update from Jennifer. "*When I opened the door, N157 tore out of the trap and ran up the hillside. There*

was absolutely no indication of his handicap. He was able to move at great speed with a completely normal gait and vacated the area in a few short minutes. What a bear!"

$$\ggg\lll$$

N157's ability to run proves that it's easy to make assumptions about wildlife based on appearance. The biologists don't know whether N157's survival is directly related to his urban environment, but it is a possibility. The team still does not know if Asheville's bears are growing bigger or producing more offspring as a result of living in an urban area. That data is being collected and will have to be analyzed. What the scientists do know is that the bear population in and around Asheville appears to be doing well. The team

Clockwise from left: Sam, Henry, Mason, Lyla, Abby, and Bodie spend some time with N157 before he receives the drug that will wake him.

BearWise

www.bearwise.org

North Carolina, Alabama, Arkansas, Florida, Georgia, Kentucky, Louisiana, Mississippi, Missouri, Oklahoma, South Carolina, Tennessee, Texas, Virginia, and West Virginia all participate in the BearWise program.

hopes that in the next couple of years, they will generate results that answer many of their questions and establish a base line for local bear behavior. As human-bear interactions increase with ongoing real estate development in and around Asheville, the bear study team continues their important work. Every day they share what they know with the public and encourage residents to support bears by keeping them wild.

"We want to show people that these animals are wonderful and can be enjoyed by everyone," says Colleen, "and we aren't the only state in the South with increased black bear activity." As part of a new initiative called BearWise (bearwise.org), North Carolina has joined forces with fourteen southeastern states to raise awareness about the black bear population. Neighborhoods and businesses can choose to become certified by BearWise as places dedicated to keeping bears wild and reducing conflicts between people and their neighborhood wildlife.

"Our goal," Colleen adds, "is to provide resources that solve problems, and to encourage communities to get involved. When people have the facts, they don't have to be afraid."

SIX WAYS TO BE BEARWISE

1. **Never feed or approach bears.** Feeding bears (intentionally or unintentionally) trains them to approach homes and people for more food. Bears will defend themselves when they get too close to people, so don't risk your safety and theirs!
2. **Secure food, garbage, and recycling.** Food and food odors attract bears, so don't reward them with easily available food or garbage.
3. **Remove bird feeders when bears are active.** Birdseed and other grains have a high calorie content, making them attractive to bears. It is very difficult to keep bird feeders and spillage safe from these animals.
4. **Never leave pet food outdoors.** Feed outdoor pets portion sizes that will be completely eaten during each meal, and securely store these foods so nothing is available to bears.
5. **Clean and store grills.** After you use an outdoor grill, clean it thoroughly, making sure that all grease and fat is removed. Store cleaned grills and smokers in a secure area that bears can't reach.
6. **If you see bears in your area, tell your neighbors.** Share news with friends and neighbors about recent bear activity and tell them how to avoid bear conflicts. Bears have adapted to living near people; are you willing to adapt to living near them?

HOW TO BEHAVE IN A BEAR ENCOUNTER

- Do not approach the bear.
- Avoid looking the bear in the eye. This is a sign of aggression in the animal kingdom.
- From a safe distance, make loud noises: shout, or bang pots and pans together (to scare the bear).
- After the bear leaves, remove potential attractants such as garbage, birdseed, or pet food.
- Ask neighbors to remove attractants and to stay alert for bear activity.

WEB RESOURCES

If you "like" bears and want to learn more about Asheville's urban/suburban black bear population, visit the study's Facebook page to meet more radio-collared bears and the residents working with the team: facebook.com/urbanbearstudy.

Are you curious about other ways to become a citizen scientist? Find projects or ways to participate, and connect with others in your city, neighborhood, or maybe even your own backyard, at iNaturalist.org.

For more information about all of North Carolina's wildlife, visit ncwildlife.org.

GLOSSARY

apex predator a predator at the top of the food chain that is not preyed upon by any other animal.

biological carrying capacity the maximum number of individuals of a species that can exist in a habitat indefinitely without threatening other species in that habitat.

delayed implantation a reproductive strategy in which the embryo (blastocyst) does not immediately implant in the uterus after sexual reproduction has created the zygote, but is maintained in a state of dormancy until the animal is healthy enough to give birth.

global positioning system (GPS) a satellite-based navigation system.

histoplasmosis a potentially life-threatening respiratory disease caused by or associated with decaying bat guano or bird droppings.

hyperphagia a period of time during which bears fatten up for the winter denning season.

immunocontraception birth control method that wildlife biologists can use to stabilize or reduce animal population numbers.

invasive species a plant, animal, or pathogen that is non-native (or alien) to the ecosystem under consideration and whose introduction causes or is likely to cause harm.

mast fruit of the forest, such as berries and nuts that fall from trees and bushes.

murmuration a flock of starlings.

Passive Integrated Transponder (PIT) tag a digital microchip identifier injected beneath the skin of an animal.

radio collar a battery-powered wildlife collar used to track an animal remotely.

social carrying capacity the maximum number of a species that a human population is willing to tolerate.

yearling a young bear between one and two years of age.

NOTES

1. A CLOSE ENCOUNTER

Information in this chapter came from personal interviews with Colleen Olfenbuttel, Nicholas Gould, Jennifer Strules, Dr. Christopher DePerno, and Bill Risdall.

20 *"N057 stayed with her cub"*: email correspondence with Colleen Olfenbuttel, March 3, 2017, 8:16 a.m.

2. CONSEQUENCES OF CONSERVATION

Unless otherwise noted, information in this chapter came from personal interviews with Colleen Olfenbuttel, Nicholas Gould, and Dr. Christopher DePerno.

26 *depended on bears for meat*: Jane Krupnick, "Black Bear: North Carolina Wildlife Profiles," ncwildlife.org; accessed April 15, 2017.

28 *four billion*: Tom Horton, "Revival of the American Chestnut," americanforests.org; accessed April 16, 2017

31 *Adult bears do not*: "Black Bears (Ursus americanus) Facts," dgif.virginia.gov; accessed April 16, 2017

36 *Tree marking*: "About Black Bears," massaudubon.org; accessed April 20, 2017.
It is uncertain: "Living with Wildlife: Black Bears," wdfw.wa.gov; accessed April 20, 2017.
The current world record: Krupnick, "Black Bear: North Carolina Wildlife Profiles."

3. A WORLD GOING WILD

43 *11.2 billion by the year 2100*: "World Population Projected to Reach 9.7 Billion by 2050," United Nations Department of Economic and Social Affairs, un.org; accessed June 21, 2017.
"Living ghosts": Elizabeth Soumya, "The Leopards of Mumbai: Life and Death Among the City's 'Living Ghosts,'" theguardian.com, November 26, 2014.
thirty-five flesh-and-blood leopards: Richard Conniff, "Learning to Live with Leopards," ngm.nationalgeographic.com, November 10, 2015.
176 attacks on humans: Joe Shute, "Leopards of Mumbai—the big cats living alongside locals in India," telegraph.co.uk, November 5, 2016.

44 *forty square miles*: Conniff, "Learning to Live with Leopards."
the area of New York City's Central Park: Soumya, "The Leopards of Mumbai."
300,000 Mumbaikars: Maria Thomas, "A Leopard Loitering Around a Mumbai Suburb Got Clicked by Biology Professor," qz.com, October 21, 2016.
appeared around 1919: "The Coywolf and Its New York City Habitat," pbs.org, January 22, 2014.
the term is inaccurate: Roland Kays, telephone interview with the author, January 24, 2017.
"Over time": Ibid.

47 *"They're absolutely everywhere"*: Kenneth Chang, "In Hawaii, Chickens Gone Wild," nytimes.com, April 6, 2015.
twenty thousand on the island: Diane Ako, "Feral Chicken Problem Invades Oahu," hawaiinewsnow.com; accessed January 15, 2017.

47 *James Cook explored:* Chang, "In Hawaii, Chickens Gone Wild."

48 *people as "subordinate":* "Preventing Conflicts with Wild Turkeys," mass.gov; accessed May 5, 2017.
   In 1972 they trapped: Yoni Appelbaum, "Why Wild Turkeys Hate the Wild," theatlantic.com, November 25, 2015.

50 *In the late nineteenth century:* Steve Carlic, "Introducing America's Most Hated Bird: The Starling," syracuse.com, September 7, 2009.
   two hundred million starlings: Ibid.
   $9 million in damages: Ibid.
   $800 million loss in agricultural: Ibid.
   flocks of forty thousand: Ibid.
   In 1960: Ibid.
   In 1996: Ibid.

52 *3.5 million residents:* Gero Schliess, "Berlin 24/7: Germany's Capital Is Growing at an Alarming Speed," dw.com, January 15, 2017.
   25 percent of Berliners: Simon Arms, "Berlin Plans Hunt of Wild Boar Invaders," theguardian.com, November 30, 2011.

54 *In 1995, five:* Sarah Zielinski, "Capybaras May Be Poised to Be Florida's Next Invasive Rodent," sciencenews.org, August 12, 2016.
   "Sightings of the animals": Ibid.
   "It's a fine line": Avianne Tan, "Capybaras, Giant Rodents Native to South America, Could Become Invasive Species in Florida," abcnews.go.com, August 24, 2016.

4. **"WHAT A BEAR!"**

Unless otherwise noted, information in this chapter came from personal interviews conducted during fieldwork on May 2, 2017.

62 *"When I opened the door":* Jennifer Strules, email correspondence with the author, May 11, 2017, 10:21 a.m.

SELECTED BIBLIOGRAPHY

Donovan, Tristan. *Feral Cities: Adventures with Animals in the Urban Jungle*. Chicago: Chicago Review Press, 2015.

Kilham, Benjamin, and Ed Gray. *Among the Bears: Raising Orphan Cubs in the Wild*. New York: Henry Holt, 2002.

Rennicke, Jeff. *The Smoky Mountain Black Bear: Spirit of the Hills*. Gatlinburg, Tenn.: Great Smoky Mountains Natural History Association, 1991.

ACKNOWLEDGMENTS/AUTHOR'S NOTE

I wish to thank the following people, who contributed their time, advice, and experience to this book: the North Carolina Wildlife Resources Commission and North Carolina State University, partners in the North Carolina Urban/Suburban Black Bear Study; Colleen Olfenbuttel, Nicholas Gould, Jennifer Strules, and Dr. Christopher DePerno; Mike Carraway, Roland Kays, Bill Risdall, Don Stutts, Rebecca Dougherty, Jessica and William Withers, and Matthew Waehner; Kim Andersen at the State Archives of North Carolina; and Mike Aday, librarian-archivist, Great Smoky Mountains National Park. An especially big "thank y'all" to Kathryn Taylor and the students of Montessori Elementary School of Asheville: Gus, Lyla, Bodie, Henry, Jackson, Mason, Abby, and Sam. Finally, to Steve Atkins, thanks for the gorgeous photography!

INDEX

A

apex predator, 44

Asheville, 1, 3, 4, 6–8, 10, 31

B

bears

    average size, 36

    body language, 28

    capture and examination, 10–13, 15–20

    caught by culvert traps, 56–58

    family structure, 14

    feeding, 30

    home ranges, 10, 37

    map of population changes, 32–33

    population statistics, 3, 26, 30, 32–33

    precautions to take, 66

    reproduction, 18

    tracking methods, 6, 8–9, 16–20, 61

    tree marking, 36

    web resources, 67

BearWise, 64

biological carrying capacity, 10

C

capybaras, in Florida, 54

chestnut blight, 26, 28

chickens, feral, in Hawaii, 47

Congdon, Elizabeth, 54

conservation efforts, 38

D

DePerno, Christopher, 4, 22

disease, 50, 61

E

ear tags, 6, 61

eastern coyote, 44–47

G

garbage, as bear attractant, 3

Gering, Eben J., 47

Gould, Nicholas, 4, 25

GPS, 6

H

hibernation, 6

hunting, 3, 30–31, 37–38

hyperphagia, 4

I

immunocontraception, 41

invasive species, 50

K

Kays, Roland, 44

L

leopards, in Mumbai, 43–44

M

mast, 34

N

North Carolina State University, 4, 44

North Carolina Urban/Suburban Black Bear Study

    about, 4

    mortality factors, 38

    origins of, 31

    study objectives, 34

North Carolina Urban/Suburban Black Bear Study objectives, 34

North Carolina Wildlife Resources Commission (NCWRC), 4, 34, 38

O

Olfenbuttel, Colleen, 4, 22

P

PIT tag, 16, 61

R

radio collar, 6, 8–9, 61

S

social carrying capacity, 10

starlings, 50

Strules, Jennifer, 4, 25

study objectives, 34

T

tattoo, 6, 61

W

wild boars, in Berlin, 52

wild turkeys, in Boston, 48

SCIENTISTS IN THE FIELD
Where Science Meets Adventure

Check out these titles to meet more scientists who are out in the field—and contributing every day to our knowledge of the world around us:

Looking for even more adventure? Craving updates on the work of your favorite scientists, as well as in-depth video footage, audio, photography, and more? Then visit the Scientists in the Field website!

sciencemeetsadventure.com